CW01663635

£2.95

THE S.A.S.

~THEIR EXPLOITS TOLD IN WORDS AND PICTURES!

researched and written by

PETER NEWARK

© 1984 GRANDREAMS LTD.

Published by
GRANDREAMS LTD.,
Jadwin House, 205/211 Kentish Town Road,
London NW5.

Printed in Holland.

ISBN 0 86227 236 X

Photographs supplied by Peter Newark.
Picture credits: *Soldier Magazine* pages 9, 51, 42, 47. *Australian SAS* pages 36-37, 48-49. *SAS* pages 19,24-25, 30-31, 34-35, 44. *New Zealand Army* pages 40-41. All remaining pictures **Peter Newark.**

Contents

S.A.S.

In our first book about the SAS we told in detail about how an SAS trooper is selected, trained, and armed. We also described some of the thrilling exploits in SAS history, including the world-famous siege-breaking operation at the Iranian Embassy, London, in the spring of 1980 when the SAS were seen in action on our television screens.

In this new book we relate other exploits and operations in which the SAS have proved themselves to be the world's best all-purpose, all-weather warriors. Who else could have stormed the towering Green Mountain in Oman in so short a time?

Founded in 1941 by David Stirling, its first commander, the SAS served with daring and distinction in North Africa and Europe throughout World War Two.

Below: David Stirling (standing), founder of the SAS, with a unit of his desert raiders.

Disbanded in 1945 the SAS regiment was revived in 1947 as a Territorial unit. When a special jungle force was required to fight in Malaya, 22 SAS came into being in 1952, and this has remained the regular operational regiment; 21 and 23 SAS are the Territorial regiments. SAS units have fought all over the world: in the jungle, the desert, in mountain country, and the wind-swept wilderness of the Falkland Islands. The SAS are specialists in reconnaissance, undercover work, anti-terrorist operations, and ambush. The Regiment has served in Northern Ireland since 1969. In the autumn of 1983 SAS sprang an ambush and shot dead two IRA gunmen and wounded a third. A few months later the SAS swooped by helicopter and foiled a robbery by an

armed terrorist gang in South Armagh.
Being an elite force, only the very best men are selected for service in the SAS. Volunteers are drawn from other regiments. The training course is so tough, so demanding that 90 per cent of the volunteers fail to get through. Those who pass the entire course with flying colours are 'badged' – presented with the coveted SAS beige beret and winged dagger badge bearing the motto:

'Who Dares Wins.'

It takes three years to train an SAS trooper, and during that time he will most probably have gained active service experience. The Regiment is expected to go into action anywhere in the world at 24 hours notice. Over

When David Stirling was captured in 1943, his old adversary, Field-Marshal Rommel, the 'Desert Fox' paid him tribute with this comment:

"Thus the British lost the very able and adaptable commander whose desert group caused us more damage than any other British unit of equal strength."

Below: Two men of a four-man SAS patrol make a compass check during an exercise in Denmark.

the last thirty years the reputation and military influence of the SAS has given rise to SAS regiments in the Australian and New Zealand armies.

From trooper to commanding officer, the SAS is a unique regiment of individuals, all with absolute trust in each other, all extremely proud to be one of this hand-picked band of brothers. There is no class nonsense. Officers call their men by Christian names and answer to 'Boss' or 'Chief'. An SAS officer expects a great deal from his men, and the men expect the officer to measure up to them in every way and then give a bit extra. SAS operations require an officer, carrying the same equipment as his men, to outshoot and outmarch them under the toughest of conditions.

The Phantom Major

David Stirling, six feet six inches tall, came from a distinguished Scottish family of soldiers and adventurers. He wanted to be the first man to climb Mount Everest and was training for the event in the Rocky Mountains when the outbreak of war in 1939 brought him back home to join the Scots Guards and later the Commandos.
During the early parachute training of the fledgling SAS two men fell to their death when their canopies failed to open, due to a faulty clip on the static line that should have pulled open the parachute as the men jumped from the aircraft.
Stirling immediately stopped the jumps and set about detecting the deadly fault in the equipment. He then went up himself to test a new type of clip .
It proved successful!
The first SAS airborne operation in North Africa, against a German airfield in November 1941, proved a failure. Sand storms caused the raiders to be dropped in the wrong place.

Stirling decided to switch from airborne to land-launched attack, his men being transported to and from their objective areas by the trucks of the Long Range Desert Group.
The first SAS landborne strike proved a spectacular triumph. Twenty-four enemy aircraft destroyed at Tamit without a single SAS casualty.
WHO DARES WINS
The increasing success of his small elite force moved Stirling to create the unit's own badge and motto.
Stiring hand-picked all his men. They were a daring, dangerous and amazingly durable bunch of hard men. David Sillito was a fine example. Separated from his group after a raid, Sillito walked alone 180 miles through the desert, without food and only a little water . . .
After eight days of forced marching he reached safety and made a full recovery from his ordeal.

Coolness under fire was another SAS requirement. One night on a desert road behind enemy lines, Stirling's truck ran into an Italian ambush.
Stirling's driver, "Flash" Gibson, lived up to his nickname. He slammed down his foot and gunned the truck through the barricade . . .
The raiders got clean away without a single injury!
When jeeps first arrived in North Africa from America, Stirling immediately equipped his force with fifteen of the sturdy little vehicles, which he armed with machine-guns.
Now independent of the LRDG transport, Stirling's SAS struck swifter and harder than before, racing their jeeps between lines of enemy aircraft, shooting and hurling grenades.

During one such moonlight attack Stirling's jeep was knocked out of action . . .
But David was unhurt and another jeep came to his rescue and picked him up.

Because of the continuing success of his hit-and-run raids Stirling became known to the Germans as the "Phantom Major" . . .
And a special patrol of 500 men was detailed to hunt him down.

Stirling's amazing luck finally ran out in January 1943 when the German patrol managed to surround him and some of his men in a ravine.

A few days later, at night, Stirling made a daring break for freedom and escaped into the desert.

He made his way through the wilderness with the aid of a compass disguised as a button, a device he carried for just such a situation as this.
After several days in the desert Stirling was betrayed by an Arab who informed the Italians of his whereabouts. Again he was captured.
This time he was flown to a POW Camp in Italy.
After four escape attempts in Italy he was transferred to the top-security POW Camp of Colditz in Germany.
David Stirling remained in Colditz for the rest of the war in Europe, but his dynamic creation the SAS grew in size and success, destroying hundreds of aircraft, bridges, railways and other vital objectives.

S.A.S.

War in Europe

After its foundation in the North African campaign of World War Two — in which the SAS destroyed some 400 enemy aircraft on the ground — an expanded SAS saw plenty of action in the Greek Islands, in Sicily and Italy, and with the Allied invasion of France, became operational in North-West Europe.

"L Detachment" of the early days in the desert had grown into the 1st SAS, commanded by the legendary "Paddy" Mayne, and in 1943 a new regiment was formed, 2nd SAS, commanded by David Stirling's brother, Bill. This gave rise to the leg-pulling belief that SAS stood for "Stirling and Stirling." By the time the invasion of Europe came in June 1944 the SAS had Brigade strength and included Free French and Belgian parachute squadrons.

In Europe and Italy the daring warriors of the winged dagger carried out special raids and sabotage missions,

A bridge vital to the Germans is blown-up by the SAS in France during the allied invasion.

Left: *During World War Two, SAS soldiers made many dangerous night jumps into enemy territory.* Right: *At the wheel is SAS Major Ian Fenwick killed in action behind enemy lines in France, 1944.*

The War in Europe

captured key bridges and airfields, and armed and trained Resistance fighters. Mostly operating behind enemy lines, SAS units were always in the sharp end of the battle.

In July 1944 Captain Bradford, two sergeants and two Resistance men were riding in a jeep loaded with explosives on a country road near the French village of Lucy. Suddenly, they ran into a parked German troop convoy. It was too late to turn about and flee, so Bradford decided to speed on and shoot their way through. With machine-guns blazing the SAS ran the gauntlet of heavy fire from the long line of trucks. By the time they got past, Bradford and a Frenchman were dead and all the others were wounded. Then, just out of sight of the Germans the riddled jeep conked out. The three survivors made off into the woods and managed to reach safety.

In September 1944 an SAS parachute unit operating behind enemy lines in Belgium came into possession of a map that detailed German divisional strength on the Somme. Housed in a barn the SAS men began to transmit the vital information to GHQ when a group of Germans arrived on a tracked vehicle.

In the gunfight that ensued, the barn was set alight. Taking advantage of the thick smoke screen generated by the fire, the SAS troopers managed to slip away and hide in a field while the Germans searched for them in vain. They completed sending their message to GHQ, information that proved of great importance in waging war in that area.

In December 1944 a squadron of 2nd SAS commanded by Major Roy Farran was sent to Italy to organise, train and lead Partisan forces against the Germans. Farran and his men whipped the motley crowd of Italian guerrillas and escaped Russian POWs into shape and

The SAS destroyed some 400 enemy aircraft in land raids on airfields during the North African campaign of World War Two.

The War in Europe

in the spring of 1945 launched a surprise attack on the HQ of the German 51 Corps at the village of Albinea in the Po Valley. This HQ — housed in the Villa Calvi and the Villa Rossi — had a strength of 300 and controlled a large area of the German front.

Farran divided his force. He would lead a party of ten SAS men and twenty Italians against the Villa Calvi, and the second group of ten SAS and fifty Italians and Russians, led by Captain Lees, would attack the Villa Rossi. Having approached close to the Villa Calvi without detection, the raiders were challenged by sentries standing outside the building. A burst from an SAS Bren gun mowed them down. Then all hell broke loose.

The Bren gun burst "triggered automatic fire from every direction," recorded Farran. "The night was shattered by the rattle of machine-guns. I heard the harsh rasp of Spandau [German machine-gun]... Bullets whistled over our heads... Even mortars added their thuds to the general racket and, between the rattle of small arms fire at Villa Calvi above, I heard the thump of a bazooka."

The bazooka (an American anti-tank weapon) had been used to blast down the villa door. In charged the raiders and fought their way to the Operations Room, killing the Germans who stood in the way and driving others up the stairs. It was a savage close-quarter fight, with the Germans tossing grenades down the stairs. The SAS piled up maps, documents, files and furniture in the middle of the Operations Room, poured petrol over the heap and set it alight. Not until the flames had engulfed the room did the raiders withdraw, leaving the blazing villa lighting up the night sky.

At the Villa Rossi the Lees group met even harder opposition. The Germans retreated to the upper floor and maintained heavy fire against the invaders, who

Left*: Some of Skorzeny's tough glider-commandos who crash-landed on a mountain top to rescue Benito Mussolini.* Right*: The legendary R.B. 'Paddy' Mayne who became commanding officer of the SAS after David Stirling was captured in 1943.*

The War in Europe

attempted several times to rush the main staircase but were always repulsed. Captain Lees and the Italian Partisan leader were badly wounded and several others killed. Having set the Villa Rossi alight the Lees party withdrew, carrying their wounded with them. Evading German search parties on the way, the combined SAS-Partisan force marched for 22 hours without pause until reaching safety.

The raid was highly successful. Sixty Germans, many of them staff officers, had died in the battle, including the Chief of Staff, and the HQ destroyed with all its documents, a great loss to the enemy. The raiders suffered three killed, all SAS, eight wounded and six captured by the Germans. It was exactly the type of operation that David Stirling would have approved.

The continuing activities of the SAS so angered Hitler that he issued a directive that all captured commandos and SAS be executed and a number of them died while in German hands. One of them was Philip Pinckney, an officer of 2nd SAS. In the summer of 1943 he was parachuted on to the Brenner Pass in the central Tyrolese Alps, where he blew up the railway tunnel, a vital link between Germany, Austria and Italy. Pinckney was captured and shot by the Gestapo.

One German officer in particular who held no hatred for the SAS was Major Otto Skorzeny; indeed, he admired and respected their daring and military enterprise. Skorzeny was ordered to raise a commando unit for special operations behind enemy lines. He studied reports of SAS raids and learned from them. He hand-picked his men and trained them vigorously. Each man had to be a parachutist, a swimmer, a rock climber, a linguist, explosive expert and crackshot, and be able to drive and repair any type of motor vehicle.

A Vickers machine-gun crew of 2nd SAS in the Castino region of Northern Italy during World War Two.

The War in Europe

Skorzeny accomplished one of the greatest commando raids of the war — the airborne rescue of Benito Mussolini from a mountain-top prison — an exploit that won the admiration and professional approval of the SAS. Enemies they were, but Skorzeny and David Stirling came from the same tribe. The Skorzeny story is worthy of inclusion in a book about the SAS.

When Italy surrendered to the Allies on 8 September 1943 Mussolini, the former dictator and ally of Hitler, was being held captive in a secret place, prior to being handed over to the victorious Allies, or executed by his own people. Hitler ordered Skorzeny to locate and rescue his loyal friend Mussolini. But where was the ex-dictator being held?

Fortunately for Skorzeny the answer was not long in coming. He intercepted a coded message to the Italian Ministry of Interior: "Security Measures Around Gran Sasso Completed. Cueli." Skorzeny already knew that General Cueli was the man responsible for Mussolini's safety. The Gran Sasso was the highest peak in the Apennines range.

After conducting a personal aerial reconnaissance of the area Skorzeny came to the right conclusion. The only spot in the Gran Sasso region where a state prisoner with a company of guards could be housed was a winter sports hotel, the Campo Imperatore, built 6,000 feet up on a sloping crag. It could only be reached by a funicular railway, and that could be easily cut to give the hotel complete isolation. It seemed an impregnable prison. Skorzeny discovered that the whole area had been sealed off with Italian troops and 250 were lodged in the hotel itself.

Skorzeny outlined his plan for the raid. A parachute drop was out of the question, so gliders carrying paratroops and his commandos would be used. The gliders would be required to crash-land on the

Left: *Otto Skorzeny, the German commando officer much admired and respected by the SAS.* Right: *Otto Skorzeny, behind Mussolini, escorts the ex-dictator to the little plane that would fly him off the mountain top.*

The War in Europe

small rock-studded shelf that sloped like a ski-run! Having freed Mussolini, three special Heinkel planes would land on the crag and fly off the ex-dictator and his saviour.

The German military experts that Skorzeny consulted called the plan impossible; it could not be carried out successfully. Skorzeny, they said, would be flying to his doom. "There are some things you can't work out with a slide rule," Skorzeny told his commandos. "That's where the experts could be wrong. The safer the enemy feel, the better our chances of catching him unawares." The SAS would have agreed with that statement.

Skorzeny and his 100 sky raiders set off on their daring mission on the afternoon of 12 September 1943 in twelve gliders towed by planes; four of the gliders never made it to the objective. Skorzeny's glider was the first to crash-land on the rocky ledge, and he was the first out, running the 20 yards to the hotel with his commandos at his heels. The suddenness of the assault stunned the guards, who were further confused by the appearance of an Italian general with the Germans, calling on them to lay down their arms. Skorzeny had thought it a good idea to take the pro-German General Soletti along on the mission.

No shots were fired. The huge commando leader (like David Stirling he was very tall and like "Paddy" Mayne he was very strong) barged his way through the Italian soldiers who barred his progress. His commandos using gun butts and fists in dealing with any guards who looked like resisting. Skorzeny soon found Mussolini, as startled as his guards at the dramatic manner of his rescue.

Skorzeny now confronted the Italian commander of the hotel garrison and demanded his immediate surrender "to avert senseless bloodshed." The commander surrendered.

Una información especial

"¡Mani in alto!" gritó Otto Skorzeny, jefe que dirigió
del Duce, a la guardia del hotel alpino. Asustados y
carabinieri obedecieron inmediatamente esta

La liberación de M

Skorzeny's commandos rush the hotel in which Mussolini was being held captive. Front page of *Signal*, German propaganda magazine.

The War in Europe

So far, so good. Then things began to go wrong. The escape plan involving the three Heinkels had to be abandoned. The only way left to get Mussolini off the peak was to land a tiny Stork observation plane on the sloping crag.

The pilot performed an aerial miracle in setting the plane down safely on the small rock-strewn patch. Then, overloaded with the substantial weight of Mussolini, Skorzeny and the pilot the frail Stork prepared to take off. Twelve men hung desperately on to the plane, restraining it until the engine had reached full power. They let go and the Stork catapulted forward over the edge of the crag and plunged in a nose-dive to the valley floor! With considerable skill and good fortune the pilot pulled the plane into level flight and landed at Rome. From there the commando leader and his important charge flew to Germany.

Overnight Otto Skorzeny had become a national hero. Hitler promoted him and showered him with medals. Winston Churchill, the British Prime Minister, voiced Allied admiration of the exploit. "It was a stroke of great daring," he said at the time, then, with our own SAS-Commando operations in mind, he added: "It shows there are many possibilities of this kind open in modern warfare." Colonel Skorzeny carried out other special operations and survived the war with honour.

With the Allied advance over the Rhine, the SAS spearheaded the final offensive, capturing key bridges and airfields and cutting the enemy lines of communications. By the end of the war in Europe, May 1945, the SAS Brigade had inflicted nearly 8,000 casualties on the enemy and captured some 20,000, suffering 330 casualties themselves in the process. Having served with great distinction the SAS Brigade was disbanded in October 1945.

Mirbat, in the Oman, where ten SAS soldiers fought off hundreds of rebel guerrillas.

S.A.S.

Desert Warriors

The Jebel Akhdar (Green Mountain) rises sheer out of the Oman desert to a height of 10,000 feet. Its rocky, almost vertical walls support a plateau some ten by twenty miles. There are a number of twisting paths to the top but these tracks could be easily defended by a handful of determined men against an army. As a military stronghold it had been impregnable for a thousand years. In late 1958 this natural, formidable fortress was occupied by a strong force of well-armed, crackshot Omani rebels opposed to the Sultan of Muscat and Oman.

Britain had a long-standing treaty with Muscat and when the Sultan requested military assistance to rid his country of rebels backed by Egypt and Saudia Arabia, the British government responded by first sending military advisors to train loyal Omani soldiers, then small units of British regular troops. The British-Omani force drove the rebels (600-strong) to seek refuge on the Green Mountain. And neither land assault nor air attack by the RAF could defeat or drive the enemy from his towering stronghold.

But the situation could not be left like that. The plateau had to

cleared. In this the British government had to be very careful. A full-scale military operation was out of the question lest it triggered world-wide condemnation against British "imperialism" and "aggression". International politics demanded that the task be done as quietly and as quickly as possible — in weeks rather than months — with minimum casualties to the assaulting force. Only the SAS were capable of carrying out this "mission impossible."

At that time 22 SAS was on active service against Communist guerrillas in the Malayan jungle. "D" Squadron was pulled out of that campaign and sent to the Oman to storm the Green Mountain. The troopers arrived in the desert midway through November 1958 and were immediately put through an intensive retraining programme in mountain warfare.

It says much for the flexibility and toughness of the

SAS soldier that, in so short a time, he can switch from jungle fighter to desert warrior; that he can swiftly acclimatise from the steam-heat of the swampy rain forest to the dry, burning desert where the nights turn bitterly cold. Jungle fighting called for close-range combat, the shotgun being the favoured SAS weapon. In the desert, with a 30-mile visibility, the shotgun gave way to high-powered rifles.

"D" Squadron soon learned two basic lessons. While gaining a toehold on the lower reaches of the mountain in daylight, a corporal was shot dead by a sniper. Lesson one: the hill tribesmen were marksmen. Lesson two: operate only at night. Two troops, led by Captain Walker and guided by a local sheik, climbed a steep track 7,000 feet on the north side of the mountain and managed to reach the lower rim of the plateau undetected. The rebel lookouts being lax in that they believed no enemy would dare attempt to scale the mountain at night. At this point they did not realise that the SAS soldier is no ordinary

adversary.

Having reached the top, Walker's small force ran into opposition. Some fifty rebels, armed with rifles and machine-guns advanced against the position held by Company Sergeant Major Hawkins and nine men. The SAS held their fire until the enemy reached almost pointblank range, then they opened up with full firepower, killing ten rebels and driving the rest to safety. Captain Walker was leading a rope-climbing party up a sheer cliff when tribesmen started shooting down at him. Walker continued climbing the rope until he was near enough to toss a grenade amongst the rebels, then he and his men swarmed over the top putting the enemy to flight.

With a foothold established on the plateau the SAS called in an air strike and RAF Venoms blasted the enemy with rocket and cannon fire. As the days passed, the SAS commander came to realise that he did not have enough men to hold the captured ground, and also to probe the enemy defences and launch a final assault. A troop of Life Guards, in the role of infantry, was brought in to hold the base and free the SAS for patrol and reconnaissance. Meanwhile, "A" Squadron 22 SAS was flown in from Malaya to join "D" Squadron.

The final assault on the Jebel Akhdar was made on the more difficult south side — a 9,000 feet night climb that took ten exhausting hours to complete. Each man carried sixty pounds of equipment, mostly ammunition. Donkeys were used to carry radio sets and machine-guns. Some of the donkeys became so exhausted by the long, arduous climb that they had to be carried themselves by the SAS!

The sudden appearance of the British troops on the plateau so surprised the enemy that he either surrendered or fled down the mountain, leaving behind large quantities of arms and ammunition. The operation to conquer the Green Mountain had taken six weeks. A brilliant feat of arms. Seven members of the SAS received decorations for their part in the campaign and six others were Mentioned in Dispatches.

Early in 1964 "A" Squadron 22 SAS was sent to Aden (situated on the opposite corner of the Arabian peninsula to Oman) as part of RADFORCE to fight the "Red Wolves of Radfan." Aden, vitally placed at the entrance of the Red Sea, had been a British colony for 25 years. The port of Aden was an important trading centre. Trouble had been brewing for years between Aden and neighbouring Yemen, the latter supported and encouraged by Egypt and the Soviet Union. Egyptian and Yemeni agents working in Aden managed to persuade the fierce hill tribesmen — the "Red Wolves" — of the Radfan Mountains to start a guerrilla war against British interests and Aden troops.

RADFORCE, a combined strike force of brigade strength that included units of the Royal Marine Commando, the Parachute Regiment and several other regiments, was sent to penetrate the rugged Radfan and bring the insurgent tribesmen under the control of the Federal government. No easy task. The Radfan rebels were hard men, good fighters, and crackshots. The first operational casualties to RADFORCE were suffered by a nine-man SAS

Left: *A German patrol looking for signs of SAS activity. During the desert campaign of World War Two the Germans assigned a special force to combat the SAS.* Below: *A desert sandstorm like this put a stop to all operations in the North African campaign of World War Two.*

reconnaissance patrol commanded by Captain Robin Edwards.

Dropped at night by helicopter behind enemy positions in the Wadi Taym region, the patrol kept an eight-hour watch on rebel movements in a nearby hillside village until it was discovered by a shepherd who gave the alarm and sparked off a day-long battle. Pinned down by extremely accurate fire, the patrol called in the RAF for continual rocket strikes. Despite the effectiveness of these air attacks (at times only 25 yards from the SAS position), fifty howling Red Wolves charged at dusk and although the tribesmen were repelled, Trooper Warburton was killed and two men wounded in the close-quarter fight.

As darkness fell, Captain Edwards decided to break out of their death trap. Charging shoulder to shoulder, firing from the hip, the desperate SAS went hell-for-leather at the enemy. Edwards was fatally shot in the stomach and ordered his men to "Get out of it, and leave me alone." The survivors hacked a path through the tribesmen with rifle butts, bayonets, boots and bare fists.

During the ensuing eight-hour trek through enemy territory to base camp the SAS patrol was trailed by more Red Wolves. Despite a severe leg injury, Lance-Corporal Baker and a wounded trooper fought a series of rearguard actions until the tribesmen gave up the chase. Baker was awarded the Military Medal and Captain Edwards was Mentioned in Dispatches.

The Aden campaign of 1964-67 also saw the SAS taking part in dangerous anti-terrorist operations in the city of Aden. This called for undercover work with the SAS men wearing Arab dress. The men were specially selected for their "Arab" looks and their ability to speak Arabic. They were trained to quick-draw a Browning

automatic pistol from the folds of their Arab robes and shoot accurately. These squads hunted down Egyptian-trained assassins and terrorists who threw bombs, the latter known to the SAS as "Cairo Grenadiers." Because of the high-risk "sudden death" situation in the crowded, narrow alley ways of Aden, the SAS mostly fired first and took prisoners second. Few prisoners were taken in these operations.

The SAS returned to Oman in 1970 to aid the Sultan's forces against a Communist-armed insurrection in the country's Dhofar province, on the border with Communist South Yemen. The SAS Squadron served under the designation of British Army Training Team (BATT), its chief duty being to train Dhofari irregulars into a fighting force capable of defeating the Yemeni-backed Communist guerrillas. As well as training the tribesmen, the SAS fought alongside them.

One SAS officer entered the Sultan's service as a contract soldier of fortune. Like a latter-day Lawrence of Arabia he spent months in the desert with his Dhofari warriors; he dressed like them, spoke like them, ate the same food and shared the same thoughts. He became a Dhofari in spirit. In 1972 this officer decided to cross the border into Yemen and destroy the army fort at Sinau, a known supply base for guerrilla activity in Dhofar. Such an operation was strictly against British military policy in the Oman; border crossings were a sensitive political issue.

But the former SAS officer was now a freelance

fighter and he went ahead with his plan. He crossed the border with 100 men and two trucks loaded with explosives and drove eighty miles to the fort. Again the element of surprise brought about a bloodless surrender of the small garrison. The raiders set the charges and swiftly withdrew. As they raced towards the border, the fort was blown to pieces. Although the raid displeased the British Commander-in-Chief, the Sultan of Oman praised the bold, successful blow against the enemy.

In July 1972 came the Battle of Mirbat, one of the greatest feat of arms in SAS history; a do-or-die stand by ten SAS (BATT) soldiers, aided by a small number of local irregulars, against some 300 well-armed guerrillas. Mirbat was a coastal town with a few Beau Geste-style mud forts. The rebels attacked at dawn on 18th July with mortars, rocket-launchers and heavy machine-guns, automatic rifles, and a 25-pounder field gun divided

SAS jeep of World War Two desert campaign. This hardy little vehicle suited the hit-and-run raiders.

between two strongpoints — the BATT House HQ and an outlying fort.

The disciplined and accurate firepower of the SAS cut down many of the enemy but still they kept closing in until the situation became desperate. When the outlying fort, which had the field gun in a gunpit manned by two SAS men and several Omanis, failed to answer Kealy's radio calls, the officer decided to visit the fort to see what was happening. He and Trooper Tobin, the team's medic, ran to the fort, zigzagging the 400 yards of open ground swept by heavy enemy fire.

When they reached the gunpit in front of the fort they found all the crew wounded. The guerrillas pressed in on the gunpit. Trooper Tobin was fatally injured and a wounded comrade killed while manning the field gun alone. Now only Kealy and a wounded trooper remained able to defend the position. The enemy closed in tighter, hurling grenades, one of which landed at Kealy's feet...but failed to explode!

Then, at the very last minute, two Strikemaster jets, responding to an earlier radio call from Kealy, screamed down and pounded the guerrillas with bombs and bullets. The enemy withdrew a little and a lull settled on the battlefield. But Kealy knew that the next assault would overwhelm the gunpit and possibly the BATT House. Fortunately another SAS unit had recently arrived the day before at Salalah, the provincial capital, some forty miles away. And when news reached the town about the attack on Mirbat, twenty-three heavily-armed SAS climbed aboard three helicopters and flew off to help their hard-pressed mates. For such a small party it boasted the fire power of an infantry company — nine General Purpose Machine Guns, four M79 grenade launchers, and each man armed with an automatic rifle.

On landing in the battle zone the relieving force deployed into two ten-men assault units and a command group. This spirited attack by fresh SAS soldiers completely turned the battle and the enemy retreated, having suffered heavy losses. SAS casualties in the Battle of Mirbat were two dead and two badly wounded. Captain Kealy was awarded the Distinguished Service Order and trooper Tobin a posthumous Distinguished Conduct Medal.

The SAS remained in the Oman until the guerrilla threat was finally eradicated in 1976. During the six years of fighting this little-known campaign about a dozen SAS soldiers were killed and three times that number were wounded.

The SAS have been in and out of the jungle for more than thirty years. They have fought two successful jungle campaigns: in Malaya against Communist guerrillas in the 1950s, and in Borneo against Indonesian forces in the 1960s. By virtue of his intensive training, his toughness of mind and body, his skill with weapons, and his pride of regiment, the SAS soldier has proved himself one of the best (if not the very best) jungle fighters of the world.

The Regiment is always ready to fly anywhere in the world and go into action. The experience gained in jungle warfare has taught the SAS many valuable lessons in combat, movement, and how to survive. The troopers may change over the years but lessons learned the hard way, the knowledge absorbed, and a tradition forged in sweat and blood, remain to serve the new warriors who proudly wear the winged dagger badge.

During the Borneo campaign (1962-66) the SAS had a training camp on the island where a new intake would undergo a gruelling four-week course in jungle warfare. From dawn to dusk the new SAS arrivals would carry heavy loads through swamps and dense thickets, enduring the stifling atmosphere of a Turkish bath. The problem of getting from point "A" to designated point "B" in a wilderness with a horizon of 100 yards was mastered by days of navigation practice from one recognisable feature to another. The exercises got tougher and the sketch maps rougher but gradually the troopers grew confident in getting about.

Combat survival lessons taught the setting of Iban (native) fish and wild pig traps, what to eat and where to get it. On survival exercises troopers were left in the jungle for four days with only a packet of biscuits and a chocolate bar. On jungle

Australian SAS in jungle training.

S.A.S. Jungle Fighters

A Naval helicopter picks up an SAS patrol in the Borneo jungle in 1965.

The Jungle Fighters

ranges their reactions were honed to razor sharpness against the merest sight of targets. During the final phase when patrols are sent out on test missions, instructors would trail them and shoot them up with live ammunition if they stepped on a track. They observed each man closely and no fault was ever too trivial to escape comment.

"These lads come here as alien beings in a hostile element," said one veteran instructor of a new intake, "and leave as superior hunting animals with a rare instinct for living and fighting in the jungle. They can smell a cigarette 200 yards away and can live off virtually nothing."

The original SAS Regiment was disbanded at the end of World War Two. In 1947 the Regiment was revived in the form of a Territorial unit, designated 21 SAS. In the late 1940s British forces were engaged in a difficult jungle campaign against Communist revolutionaries in Malaya. As these guerrillas grew in strength and influence, the British military saw a positive need for a special force trained to fight and survive in the jungle.

Major (wartime Brigadier) J.M. 'Mad Mike' Calvert was given the job of raising the new force. Calvert was an expert on guerrilla and jungle warfare. He had served with the famous 'Chindits' in Burma against the Japanese, and later, in Europe he commanded the SAS Brigade. The special unit that he raised was called the Malayan Scouts (SAS), and its members included ex-Chindits and former SAS men. Calvert also requested, and was given, a squadron of 21 SAS reservists. The Malayan Scouts operated successfully in the jungle and in 1952 the force became 22 SAS Regiment.

Throughout the 1950s the SAS served in Malaya against Communist guerrillas, a cunning foe well-versed in jungle warfare and concealment. To help them hunt the enemy the SAS recruited Iban Dyak trackers from Borneo. Learning from these native trackers, a number of SAS men became expert in following a human trail, no matter how faint. Perhaps the most notable of the British trackers was Sergeant Bob Turnbull. He befriended an Iban, Private Anak Kanyan, learned the language so that he could talk fluently to both Ibans and Malayans, and became a better tracker than his Iban teacher!

AVY
A

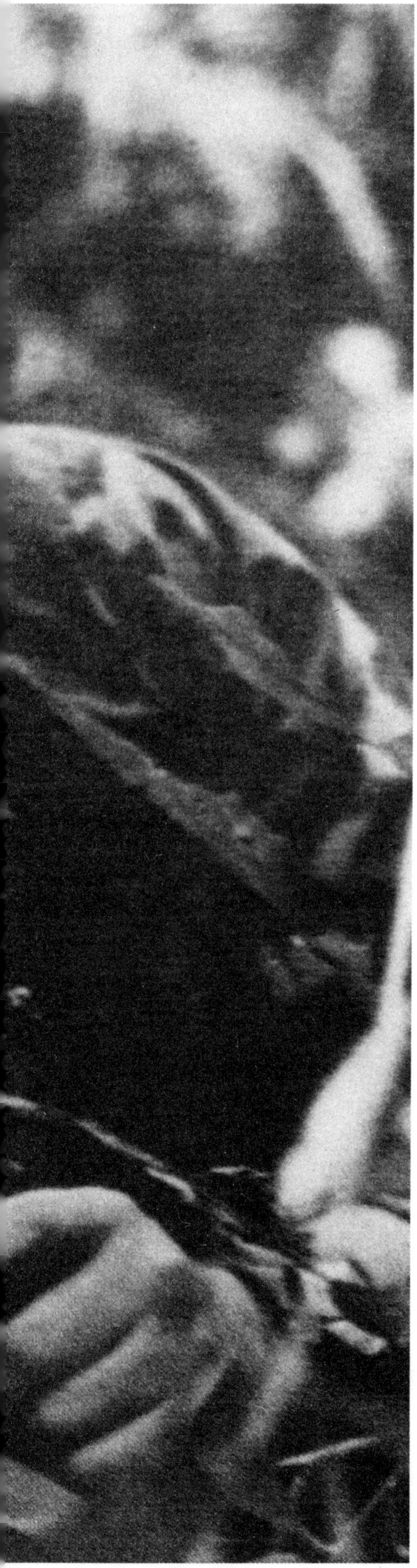

New Zealand's SAS served in the Borneo jungle campaign of the 1960s.

The Jungle Fighters

Turnbull developed the ability to shoot extremely fast and accurately, an important talent in jungle fighting. His favourite weapon being a pump-action repeater shotgun, a weapon widely used by the SAS in the Malayan campaign. Turnbull could work his shotgun so fast that three shots sounded like one.

When the new Self Loading Rifle (SLR) came into service in 1958, the SAS were among the first to be issued with the automatic weapon. And when the American M16 Armalite rifle became available in the middle 1960s it quickly became a popular SAS weapon, being much lighter, shorter, and easier to strip and clean than the SLR. The Armalite, capable of firing 800 rounds a minute, has, in various models, remained popular with the SAS. The silenced version of the Sterling sub machine-gun was a favoured weapon with the SAS to ambush track and river crossings in jungle operations.

Sergeant Turnbull became something of a legend in Malaya. One of his exploits involved trailing four guerrillas for a week. When he came upon their hut it was well guarded. Experience told him to wait for the impending rainstorm, then take them by surprise. Adverse weather means nothing to a determined SAS soldier. Timing, and winning is everything. When the rain lashed down the sentries entered the hut for cover. Turnbull, soaked to the skin, waited for his chance — then crashed into action, killing all four terrorists.

It was Sergeant Turnbull who ended the terrorist career of Ah Tuck, a guerrilla leader renowned for his skill with a Sten sub machine-gun. When finally these two confronted each other in the jungle at twenty yards, Turnbull fired his repeater shotgun with such rapidity that Ah Tuck died with his Sten gun in his hand, unfired. In 1956 Sergeant Turnbull was awarded the Military Medal for his outstanding service in Malaya.

Malaya ceased being a Crown colony in August 1957 and the successful campaign against the Communist guerrillas was virtually over, the SAS being involved in the final mopping-up operations. In 1962 President Sukarno, dictator of Indonesia (a nation of 10,000 islands), decided to start trouble in Borneo, a large island of which the greater part belonged to Indonesia. The remaining territories of

Left: *Leader of a four-man patrol of 22 SAS in the Borneo jungle during the confrontation with Indonesia in 1966.* Below: *Four-man patrol of New Zealand's SAS move warily through the Borneo bush.*

The Jungle Fighters

North Borneo, Brunei, and Sarawak were all British dependencies, and had been for a long time. Sukarno wanted all of Borneo.

At first he instigated an unsuccessful rebellion in Brunei and later began sending his regular troops raiding across the border. British forces, including the Royal Marine Commando and the Gurkhas, were ordered to Borneo and early in 1963 the SAS were established in the jungle, patrolling 700 miles of Indonesia frontier, an unmarked frontier of wild and mountainous country, mostly uninhabited.

In this campaign an SAS four-man patrol might be in the jungle for six weeks at a time. The patrol would usually move spaced out, one behind the other. The lead scout would most likely carry a repeater shotgun, next the patrol commander followed by the signaller, last man would be the team's medic carrying a General Purpose Machine Gun. The two middle men would have Armalites. Each man carried 65 pounds of equipment.

In order to take the enemy by surprise these patrols endeavoured not to use tracks, and would often not exchange a single word for perhaps twelve hours at a stretch, hand signals and instinct being enough communication. For six hours a day they would move stealthily through rain forest, 1000-yards an hour. They trod lightly leaving little or no trace of their passing. Other jungle soldiers called them 'the Tiptoe Boys.'

At regular times the SAS patrol would halt and the signaller send back a morse code report to base. Regular communication was essential. If the signal set packed up, the patrol was called off. One missed report-time was an alert, two a danger signal to base. For this reason the signaller was closely protected; if the patrol got shot up he would have the best chance of getting away with his precious equipment.

An hour before sundown the quartet would camp and eat their evening meal, often cold so as not to alert the enemy with fire smoke. Empty food packets, tins, all rubbish had to be carefully buried or carried to the end of the patrol. To leave anything, no matter how tiny, would be to invite enemy attention. A label from a coffee tin left by an Indonesian soldier brought the Gurkhas after his battalion with disastrous results for the enemy. Each man of the patrol settled down for the

SAS patrol in action during the campaign in Borneo.

The Jungle Fighters

night in a *basha* (shelter) formed from branches and a *poncho* (waterproof cape); the branches are not cut but tied down, so they can spring back into natural place when released in the morning.

The patrol would be on the move before dawn. In the jungle a clash with the enemy usually comes suddenly when two patrols confront each other. Or it comes just as suddenly when a patrol walks into a carefully prepared ambush, a speciality of the SAS who are trained to remain absolutely silent for long periods. During the Borneo campaign the SAS employed the policy of 'shoot-n-scoot' — that is, to break contact with the enemy at the earliest opportunity. An ambush party would strike and then vanish from the spot. However, it took combat experience to know exactly when to scoot.

"It's no good getting out right away," said one trooper at the time, "because you might be hammering them. But if you leave it too late they can get round the back of you."

In February 1965 Sergeant Eddie Lillico was in command of a patrol from "D" Squadron. This is the story of that patrol. A story of SAS guts and determination to survive against the odds and never surrender. The patrol walked into an ambush of Indonesian soldiers. The lead scout, Trooper Thompson was hit in the left thigh, the impact flinging him into the undergrowth near where an enemy lay concealed. They stared at each other for a moment, then Thompson fired first, killing his adversary.

Sergeant Lillico was also struck down by the initial machine-gun fire. Unable to walk, he could still use his rifle and he returned the fire. The rest of the patrol had, in SAS parlance, 'bugged-out' in accordance with 'shoot-n-scoot' orders. They made for the nearest infantry post to report contact with the enemy and to lead a stronger party back to search the area.

Thompson crawled to where Lillico was sitting and both continued firing at the enemy. Then Thompson dragged himself to another position and opened fire, hoping to fool the enemy into thinking reinforcements had arrived. Some ten minutes after the initial contact the Indonesians apparently withdrew. During the remainder of the day Thompson continued to drag himself the 2,000 yards to safety. He had applied a tourniquet to his thigh, taken

SAS in jungle training. Each man carries 65 pounds of equipment.

The Jungle Fighters

a pain-killing drug, and dressed his wound as best he could. The next day, having covered 1,000 yards, he was found by the search party and carried to a clearing where a helicopter lifted him to hospital.

Meanwhile, Sergeant Lillico, having tended his serious wounds, dragged himself a distance of 400 yards to a ridge, where he fired some signal shots to attract the attention of the search party. Bursts of automatic fire answered him...enemy fire from only a few hundred yards away! Lillico hid himself in the scrub and was both able to hear and see the Indonesians searching for him. One man climbed a tree about 40 yards away and remained there for 30 minutes in full view as he looked around.

Lillico heard an RAF helicopter, obviously searching for him. It could have been his last chance of escape but because of the enemy's nearness and the risk to the aircraft, he decided not to use his rescue radio beacon. The chopper flew away and the Indonesian observer climbed down the tree and the soldiers melted away in the jungle. The helicopter returned in the evening and this time Lillico switched on his beacon and he was winched to safety. A year later the Queen honoured his bravery with the Military Medal, and tough Trooper Thompson was Mentioned in Dispatches.

By the end of 1965 British military pressure had forced the Indonesian army to abandon its provocative border bases and concede control of the frontier to the allied forces of British, Gurkhas, and the SAS regiments of New Zealand and Australia. The war in Borneo, or the 'Confrontation,' as it was often called, ended in 1966 when Sukarno lost power in Indonesia. At the same time that Aussie troopers were serving in Borneo, the Australian SAS was on active service in Vietnam.

From 1966 to 1971 the Australian SAS in Vietnam won the admiration and respect of the American and South Vietnamese military for their bush and jungle skills (much of it learned in Borneo), especially their deep reconnaissance and ambush techniques. Australians won four Victoria Crosses in Vietnam (the V.C. is the highest British combat medal). One of them was Warrant Officer (WO) Simpson, an SAS soldier serving in the Australian Army

Australian SAS in Vietnam armed with M16 Armalite rifles.

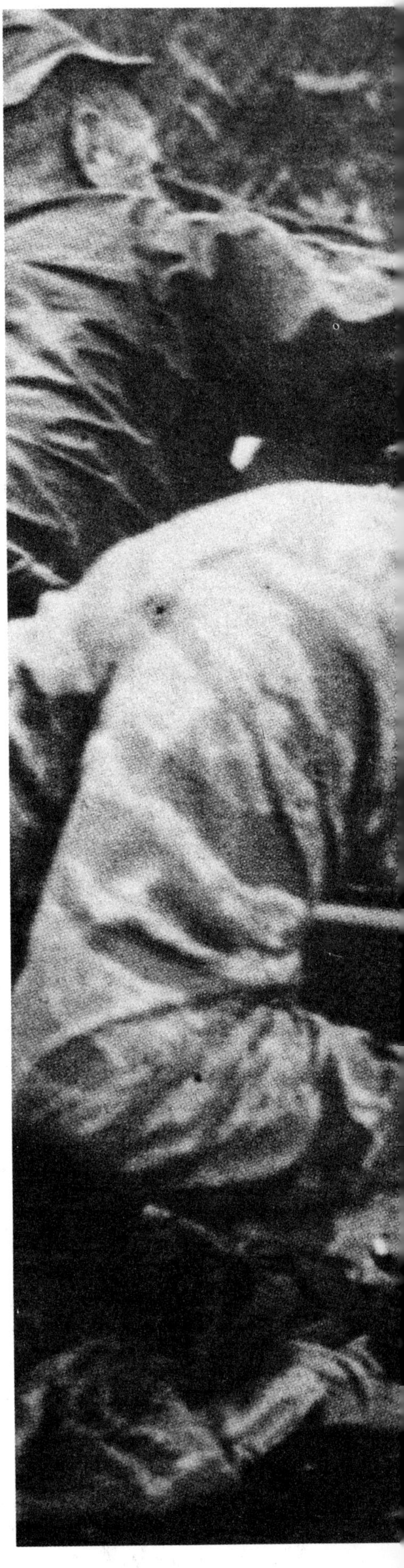

The Jungle Fighters

Training Team.

Twice in five days WO Simpson defied death to rescue wounded comrades. The first time was on 6th May 1969 when he was commanding a Special Forces mobile strike force on a search-and-clear operation in jungle country in Kontum Province. When one of his platoons became heavily engaged with the enemy he led the remainder of his company to its aid. "Disregarding the dangers involved," the V.C. citation states, "he placed himself at the front of his troops, thus becoming a focal point of enemy fire."

As the company moved forward, a fellow officer was seriously wounded and the attack began to falter. Simpson, at great personal risk and under heavy fire, moved over open ground, reached the wounded man and carried him to safety. He then crawled forward to within ten yards of the enemy and hurled grenades into their positions. As darkness fell Simpson ordered his company to withdraw. He threw smoke grenades and, carrying a wounded platoon leader, covered the withdrawal with five Vietnamese soldiers. "His leadership and personal bravery in this action," the citation records, "were outstanding."

Five days later Simpson's battalion commander was killed and a warrant officer and several Vietnamese wounded. At the risk of almost certain death, Simpson made several attempts to get to the commander's body but on each occasion was stopped by heavy fire.

Realising the position was becoming untenable and that priority should be given to saving other casualties as quickly as possible, WO Simpson alone and still under heavy fire covered the withdrawal of the wounded by personally placing himself between the wounded and the enemy. From this position he fought on and by outstanding courage and valour was able to prevent the enemy advance until the wounded were removed from the immediate vicinity.

The citation concludes: "Warrant Officer Simpson's repeated acts of personal bravery were an inspiration to all Vietnamese, United States and Australian soldiers who served with him. His conspicuous gallantry was in the highest tradition of the Australian Army." And one must add, in the very best fighting tradition of the SAS.

S.A.S.

Special Boat Squadron

On a cold dark night, 13th May 1982, eight men of Boat Troop "D" Squadron 22 SAS paddled their two-man canoes across the choppy stretch of water between West Falkland and Pebble Island. Britain was at war with Argentina, whose soldiers had invaded the Falkland Islands, a British colony in the South Atlantic.

Boat Troop was on a mission: to establish observation posts and set up a landing zone for the helicopter-borne SAS force that would strike at the enemy airstrip on Pebble Island. A daring deep-penetration operation that had its origins in the SAS hit-and-run raids in the desert campaign of World War Two.

On reaching Pebble Island the canoeists sank their craft with rocks to prevent discovery, then moved stealthily inland to set up observation posts on high ground overlooking the airstrip and Argentine troop positions. Next they established a landing zone and, in the early hours of 15th May, they set up a radio beacon that guided in three helicopters carrying 48 SAS soldiers and a naval gunfire observer.

Arriving at the high ground above the airstrip, the gunnery officer set up his laser rangefinder and through its night vision sight spotted fuel and ammunition dumps, the dug-outs, and the radar station. The gunnery expert radioed the destroyer HMS Glamorgan, *lying a mile off shore, and her 4.5 inch guns boomed out a reply. Star shells illuminated the airstrip*

Men of the SAS Boat troop training in a Gemini inflatable powered by outboard motor.

The Special Boat Squadron

for the SAS raiders. Then high explosive shells hit the enemy troop positions.

At the double, SAS four-man teams planted short-fuse firebombs in the fuel and ammunition dumps and on the aircraft parked on the strip. When Argentine soliders attempted to engage the intruders they were gunned down at short range. As the strike force withdrew to rendezvous with the helicopters, the airstrip erupted in a series of explosions.

All the raiders returned safely to HMS Hermes, *the aircraft-carrier flagship of the British Task Force. The 30-minute raid, first of its kind in this war, has been a brilliant success: 12 aircraft destroyed together with fuel and ammunition dumps, and a radar station. Only two SAS men had suffered minor wounds.*

Throughout the Falklands campaign the SAS worked hand-in-glove with the Special Boat Squadron (SBS) of the Royal Marines. SAS and SBS reconnaissance teams prepared the way for every major attack by the Task Force. These small teams would land at night by air or sea and infiltrate into, or get very near, the enemy lines, probing and penetrating for weak spots and special targets.

Hardy, silent and skilful in concealment, these scouts would hole-up for days, virtually within "spitting-distance" of Argentine troops, gathering information as to the strength, altertness and discipline of the enemy. It was an SBS team that discovered Port San Carlos — selected as the Main British beachhead — to be almost undefended.

The SAS and SBS are brothers-in-arms in a very real sense. Both are elite forces, carefully selected and highly trained for special operations. Both use similar equipment; indeed SAS Boat Troops are trained and equipped like SBS swimmer-canoeists. Both forces keep a low public profile and a closed mouth about their operations. The covert activities of the SAS and SBS are often lumped together by the Press and the public, especially in the Falklands War.

SBS recruits come from the ranks of the Royal Marine Commando. They are subjected to a rigorous training regime that embraces seamanship, navigation, underwater swimming with all kinds of equipment, beach-reconnaissance, photography, radio-communications, demolition, sabotage, and

Left: A unit of the Special Boat Squadron SAS set out on a raiding mission in the Adriatic during World War Two. *Below*: Soldiers of 22 SAS launch Gemini inflatables for a beach assault exercise in Jamaica. The SAS train in all parts of the world.

parachuting. The recruit who makes it through this extremely tough programme will pass out as a Swimmer-Canoeist Grade Three.

The SBS use all type of craft, including the two-man Klepper canoe, the inflatable Gemini powered by a 40 hp outboard motor, and the Rigid Raider craft powered by a 140 hp outboard, that skims the water at 30 knots. It is difficult to define the demarcation line between SAS and SBS activities. It is believed that the SBS deal with all operations from the high tide mark to 12 miles inland, and the SAS take on all other tasks. But the line is flexible.

Not much is known in detail about clandestine SAS and SBS operations in the Falklands campaign because they are still classified as secret. Take, for example, the mysterious case of the Royal Navy Sea King helicopter that was found burned-out and abandoned in the southern tip of neutral Chile, close to the border with Argentina and her air bases, from which aircraft equipped with Exocet missiles flew against ships of the British Task Force.

In Chile the three-man helicopter crew gave a short press conference in which the pilot explained that "We were on sea patrol and had engine failure due to adverse weather. It was not possible to return to our ship in such weather. We therefore sought refuge in the nearest neutral country." This incident gave rise to the belief that the troop-carrying Sea King had landed an SAS or SBS team with the mission to monitor and report (and probably sabotage) military aircraft flying from Argentine coastal bases to the Falklands.

The SBS of the Royal Marines has its origins in a number of special raiding units of World War Two, in particular the Royal Marine Boom Patrol Detachment, the canoe section of which carried out the famous "Cockleshell Heroes" raid against German shipping at Bordeaux in December 1942. Known as the Special Boat Squadron since 1975, it is comprised of Sections, and the initials SBS can apply to both Squadron and Section.

In World War Two the SAS had a Special Boat Section (later Squadron). Commanded by Major the Earl Jellicoe, son of the admiral, the SBS element of the SAS raider enemy-occupied territory in the Mediterranean, Adriatic and Aegean Seas, destroying ships, shore installations, and taking prisoners. These SBS raiders

The Special Boat Squadron

carried out hundreds of hit-and-run operations and in so doing tied up large numbers of enemy troops sent to garrison the troublesome area.

Jellicoe's forward base in the Aegean and the Adriatic was an innocent-looking Levantine schooner named Tewfik, *which moored in sheltered coves along the shores of neutral Turkey. In some ways the hit-and-run operations of the SBS were piratical — they captured or destroyed enemy vessels, taking booty and prisoners. These bold "buccaneers" would undertake any kind of mission that would upset, aggravate, and harm the enemy.*

Major Ian Patterson was an outstanding leader of SAS/SBS raiders. One of his exploits involved disguising himself as a priest. He received information that a party of German soldiers were to visit the Aegean island of Nisiros to take away children from the orphanage, against their wishes and to the distress of the nuns who ran the place, and remove them to Rhodes. Patterson decided to give the German kidnappers a surprise. His men took the children to safety but their luggage was left in the porch of the orphanage to deceive the Germans into thinking they were prepared to leave with them.

Two German vessels tied up at the quay and an officer and 12 armed soldiers marched up to the orphanage and were greeted by Major Patterson dressed in the vestments of a priest. He took them inside and, pulling a pistol from under his robes, ordered them to surrender. The Germans decided to fight and a close-quarter battle ensued. Other SBS men were inside and outside the building. The short but savage encounter ended with two Germans dead and seven wounded. Patterson stripped off his vestments, grabbed a Bren gun and made for the quay with two of his men. They raked the two German vessels with machine-gun fire and hurled grenades until the surviving enemy surrendered. Patterson and his victorious raiders looted the vessels of food and drink and returned by motor launch to the Tewfik.

The SBS was involved in many close-quarter fights at sea. One dark night an SBS motor launch was returning to base on the Turkish coast when the skipper pulled alongside two lighters (heavy, flat-bottomed vessels used for transporting cargo in shallow water), under the impression they had been captured by the SBS. It was a trap! The lighters were full of armed Germans.

Signaller Stephenson, his tommy-gun blazing, jumped on board one of the enemy vessels and fought his way to the bridge. Two comrades followed him. The gunfire brought a third German lighter to the spot. A shell wrecked the 20mm cannon on the SBS launch and set the craft alight. Meanwhile, Stephenson and his mates had gained control of the lighter's twin-mounted Breda machine-guns on the bridge wing and continued to fire at the enemy until they ran out of ammunition. Then they dived overboard and swam more than a kilometre to the Turkish shore. They returned to Tewfik's *anchorage riding donkeys.*

In the Falklands War Royal

Left: The Levant schooner *Twefik*, the forward base of SBS operations in the Greek Islands during World War Two, seen here moored in Turkish waters. *Below*: The SBS of the Royal Marines used a British-built hovercraft in the Borneo campaign of 1962-66. It proved effective in crossing swampland and shallow waters.

Marine SBS units were employed on raids as well as reconnaissance. Like the daring attack on the oil storage tanks situated on the western arm of Port Stanley Harbour. Launched at night from trawlers-cum-minesweepers, Rigid Raider craft carried marines and SAS troopers towards the enemy-held shore (Stanley was garrisoned by some 8,000 Argentine troops).

The plan called for the raiders to climb a small cliff and take up a position overlooking the oil tanks, which they would set alight by firing grenades into them. As the Rigid Raiders chugged slowly — and therefore as silently as possible-across the bay towards the landing point, an Argentine ship turned on its floodlights, revealing the presence of the intruders. Now the SBS coxswain opened up their throttles and the Rigid Raiders skimmed at top speed to the shore in a hail of enemy fire.

The raiders hit the shore and gained the high ground, despite enemy mortar fire. Having swiftly completed their mission, they returned to their craft and, under increasing bombardment from shore guns, raced out into the bay with shells falling all around them sending up great gouts of water. On reaching a designated beach the commando-party, carrying their wounded, marched inland to a rendezvous with helicopters and were lifted out.

In reconnaissance and reconnoitre the Royal Marine SBS — motto: "By Guile not Strength" — together with the SAS contributed greatly to victory in the Falklands.

Colonel "Paddy" Mayne

Mayne was under close arrest for striking the officer when David Stirling, seeking recruits for the original SAS in 1941, asked him to join the new unit.
On the very first raid that he led against an enemy airfield, Paddy distinguished himself. He kicked open the door of the Officers Mess...
While Mayne engaged the Germans, his men planted bombs on the aircraft...
And found they were one short. Paddy wanted a full score, so he jumped into the cockpit of the remaining plane and put it out of action by ripping away the instrument panel with his bare hands!

When Mayne's raiding party withdrew, 24 enemy planes exploded into flames.
On another occasion Paddy narrowly missed being blown to bits himself. He was driving a truck loaded with bombs when one of his men shouted a warning...
Get out, quick! A fuse is burning!
Paddy and his men jumped from the speeding truck just in time. A few seconds later the vehicle was blown to pieces!
When David Stirling was taken prisoner in January 1943, Major Paddy Mayne replaced him as commander of the 1st SAS and continued to lead his men into battle. After North Africa the SAS fought in Sicily and Italy.
During the hard fight for the Italian town of Temoli, the Germans launched a counterattack and shelled the building in which Paddy was playing billiards...
But like Drake playing bowls as the Armada approached, Major Mayne refused to be rushed and calmly went on to complete the game...

He then joined the savage close-quarter battle that raged outside.

With the Allied invasion of France the SAS became operational in North-West Europe. In order to obtain first-hand reports from British agents and French Resistance fighters, Paddy parachuted into enemy territory several times.

The military intelligence that he gathered behind enemy lines enabled the SAS to strike at vital objectives such as bridges, railways, and fuel dumps.

Throughout the war Paddy Mayne, always in the thick of battle, seemed to bear a charmed life. Like the time in Germany when he won a third bar to his DSO. Heavy enemy fire was holding up an SAS advance.

Braving a storm of bullets, Paddy went forward alone, intent on silencing the enemy strongpoints.
He cleared one house...
Then silenced another.
Paddy Mayne capped this heroic exploit by rescuing wounded comrades under heavy fire.

By the end of the war Lieutenant-Colonel R. B. Mayne was the most decorated soldier in the British Army.

When the SAS was disbanded in October 1945, Paddy returned to civilian life to resume his law career.

Ten years later he died in a car accident.

In 1969 when the SAS first saw undercover service in Northern Ireland they honoured the memory of "Colonel Paddy" by parading openly in uniform and placing a wreath on his grave.